THE HEALING
POWER
OF
CREATIVE
MOURNING

This book is possible through
the collaboration of
Warren County Philanthropic
Partnership, Indianola Public Library
and Hospice of Central Iowa.

For additional end-of-life resources, please call
(641) 842-4312 or visit www.hospiceofcentraliowa.org.

Books by Jan Yager, Ph.D. (a/k/a J. L. Barkas)

*Friendshifts®: The Power of Friendship and How It
Shapes Our Lives*
Single in America
The Help Book
Victims
Creative Time Management for the New Millennium
Business Protocol
How to Write Like a Professional
*The Vegetable Passion: A History of the Vegetarian State
of Mind*
The Cantaloupe Cat (illustrated by Mitzi Lyman)

Books by Fred Yager
Untimely Death: A Novel (with Jan Yager)

Books by Priscilla Orr
Jugglers and Tides: Poems

Books by Seth Alan Barkas
In the Great Together

Journals by Jan Yager
Personal Journal
Everything Notebook
Birthday Book
Friendship Journal

THE HEALING POWER OF CREATIVE MOURNING

Poems
by
Jan Yager
Fred Yager
Priscilla Orr
Seth Alan Barkas
Scott Yager

Copyright © 2000 by Jan Yager and Fred Yager

Cover photograph by Jeffrey Yager. Copyright © 2000 by Jeffrey Yager.
Priscilla Orrpoems reprinted with permission from *Jugglers & Tides* by Orr (Hannacroix Creek Books, 1997).

Published by Hannacroix Creek Books, Inc.
1127 High Ridge Road, PMB #110   Stamford, CT 06905-1203
Phone (203) 321-8674 Fax (203) 968-0193 e-mail: hannacroix@aol.com   www.Hannacroix.com
Printed in the United States of America.

Library of Congress Catalog Card Number: 99-73767

Cataloging-in-Publication Data (Prepared by Quality Books, Inc.)

The Healing power of creative mourning : poems by Jan Yager ...[et al.].
   -- 1st ed.
      p. cm.
     Includes bibliographical references.
     ISBN: 1-889262-46-3 (hardcover)
     ISBN: 1-889262-47-1 (trade paperback)
     PARTIAL CONTENTS: Part I, Coping with illness,
   death, and grief : poems by Jan Yager. Part II,
   Coping with war : poems by Fred Yager. Part III,
   Mourning : poems by Priscilla Orr. Part IV,
    Untitled: a poem by Seth Alan Barkas. Part V,
    Coping with the loss of a grandparent : a poem by Scott Yager.

       1. Death--Poetry. 2. Grief--Poetry.
     3. Bereavement--Poetry. 4. War-Poetry.
     I. Yager, Jan, 1948-

      PN6110.D4C74 2000   808.81'93548
                         QBI99-1195

CONTENTS

Preface   vii

Part I   1
Coping With Illness, Death, and Grief
Poems by Jan Yager
Daddy, Don't Die   3
My Daddy Died Today   7
Getting Used to Life Without My Daddy   15
I Saved a Moth Today   20
Missing You   22
Holidays Are Hard   29
Trying to Get Along with Mom   35
My Late Brother's Son Turns Thirty Today   40
Goodbye, Dr. Leeds, My Psychological Guru   45
A Post-Grief (and Angry) Second Goodbye   53
Farewell, John, John Brave Little Boy,   59
   Man-Hero to Millions
Ode to My Unborn Child   65

Part II   69
Coping With War
Poems by Fred Yager
Silenced By a Bomb   71
Cold Day in Summer   72
We Won't Go   75

Part III   77
Mourning
Poems by Priscilla Orr
An Odd Elegy for My Mom   79
Grief   81

Part IV   83
Untitled
A Poem by Seth Alan Barkas
Untitled   85

Part V   93
Coping with the Loss of a Grandparent
A Poem by Scott Yager
When Grandpa Came Over   95

Epilogue: Coping With Grief   97
Selected Bibliography   102
Resources   105
About the Authors   108

Preface
by
Fred Yager and Jan Yager

The healing power of creative mourning comes from our ability to breathe life into feelings about terminal illness, death, or loss. It works like this: someone close to you is seriously ill, dying, or dies, and that loss is so overwhelming, you're afraid to feel the pain associated with it. However, by cutting off these feelings, you're actually increasing the possibility that you are making yourself ill. Emotional understanding is the missing link in the mind-body connection. By failing to feel the pain and associating the feelings with the grief and loss, you send your body into a tailspin. Bio-chemicals that are released into your system can create havoc when uncontrolled. Chemical reactions that should have caused tears, and the cathartic cleansing of those tears, instead can cause nausea, migraines, ulcers, depression, overeating (or the opposite, loss of appetite), insomnia (or, the reverse, sleepiness or inertia), and even cancer.

Fortunately, creativity is one way to help you overcome your fear of feeling the pain associated with terminal illness, death, loss, and grief. Let's face it: nobody really likes to feel pain, except for a few masochists. But by feeling the pain, especially at the time the illness or the death of a loved one is occurring, you increase the likelihood of dealing with those feelings, and going on, without short- or long-term physical or emotional consequences. (Or, if you have put off dealing with these feelings when the illness or loss occurred, you can still gain the benefits of the emotional catharsis by feeling those feelings even if it's weeks, months, or years later.)

You might want to think of pain this way. Physical pain is the body's way of alerting you to a problem that needs attention. Emotional pain acts the same way, but the treatment for it is different. Surgery is obviously not an option for emotional pain, although it may work for physical pain. Prescription drugs are also less of an option for emotional pain since it may only cover up the symptoms of your emotional pain as well as failing to deal with its cause. Pills may help the immediate pain to temporarily go away, but you still need to deal with your emotions; for most, it is beneficial to face, feel, and overcome what's causing you to feel this emotional pain.

A way to heal emotional pain is to first feel it, then gain power over it through creativity.Creativity can help to fill the emotional void caused by a loss. It empowers you as you take that loss, whether it's because of terminal illness, death, or separation, and create something from it.That something can be a poem, an essay, a story, a painting, a drawing, or a song. Just think of all the great operatic arias, blues, rock, or country and western songs that deal with loss like Eric Clapton's mournful yet uplifting "Tears From Heaven."

Creativity is also our secret weapon against death. While all of us are going to die someday, we can all write, whether a few lines in a diary or journal, a memoir, a poem, or even a letter, creating something that will last forever.

Have you ever gone into a movie theater and found yourself moved to tears by what you see on the screen? When you come out, you actually feel refreshed, invigorated by the experience of letting yourself feel. The poems in this book are designed to have a similar effect. Each in its own way may trigger a cathartic tear or two, which will help you get in touch with the blocked emotions that could be making you sick.

Read the collection straight through or, if you are inspired to pick up a pen, or turn on your computer or your tape recorder, and write (or record) a poem of your own, follow that creative impulse, returning to this collection when you finish your own creation.

But whether or not you write your own poetry, there is a cathartic benefit to reading the poems of others. They're also meant to entertain, like a good blues ballad. So sit back and enjoy the healing power of creative mourning.

Part I

Coping With Illness, Death, and Grief
Poems by Jan Yager

Daddy, Don't Die

Daddy, don't die,
I'm not ready to say good-bye,
I need more time to get to know you
Time to share
Time to grow.

Daddy, I know you've been my father
For more than four decades
But I just now feel ready to get to know you.

Can you hang on and get better?
Will your tired, weary body begin to rejuvenate?
Alas, you are eighty plus years.
Some have not even lived as long as you,
It is true,
But for me, it has not been long enough.

I long to see you running the marathon again,
Winning in your age group,
Like you did eight years ago.
Taking your brisk walks,
Lying down to read the newspaper
And watching the news.

I long to laugh with you
And share the joys that are
And are yet to be.

Oh, Daddy, look at what time has done to you!
It's cruel and unfair
As I see you suffering,
So weak, so frail,
Just lying there.

You don't even look like my Daddy
till you smile your winning smile.
The white hair,
the freckled, wrinkled skin,
the hands so smooth and bloated
and cold,
All, alas, the signs of growing old.

I know a decade ago this happened to Grandma
But I ran from it then.
I could not bear to see her body decay
as she lay in the nursing home.

So I hid until nearly the end.
Right before the end I did see her

And she was so frail and pale,
Like you,
A shadow of the robust woman
that I once knew.

I spoke at her eulogy
But I felt the same sadness I feel now
That I did not really know Grandma
That there was a woman there that was a
stranger to me.

Oh, Daddy, I want to get to know you
 before it's too late.
I want to know so many things about your life,
What you thought when you were ten,
What you looked like,
What you ate.

I want to know your thoughts
 about recent current events,
And movies too.
I want to talk with you
The way we used to do.

You were my first love, Daddy,
I was and always will be Daddy's little girl.

And here I am wanting to take care of you
But it's supposed to be the other way around.

It made me so deeply sad after I said to you,
"It must be frustrating not to be able to
do anything about being so sick,"
And I squeezed your hand,
And you shook your head in agreement,
And then a single tear ran down
 your whitish cheek
As you said, "But my mind's still healthy."

Your will to live is extraordinary
With your feeding tube
And your malfunctioning prostate.
I am flattered that you can endure so much pain
Just to see your loving wife of fifty-four years
and your family again and again.

I want you to know, dear Dad,
we're here for you in your pain.
However long we still have with you,
The amount of time is meaningless
It is our love for you that has meaning
As you give meaning to our days.

My Daddy Died Today

My Daddy died today,
What else can I say?
My Daddy died today.

I still see him lying there
Breathing through a plastic tube
I know he is at peace now.

My Daddy died today,
What more is there to say?
My Daddy died today.

Last Saturday,
My sister, my mother, and I
together again with my Daddy.

He felt our love,
He felt our connection,
He felt he could go in peace.

This was a man
So good
So kind.

This was a man
So sweet
So hard to find.

One in a million
That was my Daddy.

And I will miss him so
But he had to go
His body gave out
But not his spirit, nor his soul.

That last time I saw him,
I had to wear plastic gloves again
Because of his pneumonia,
His third pneumonia in
Just two months.

But I grabbed his frail arm,
And held his bony hand,
And I squeezed it,
And I told him,
"We're going to be okay.
We'll miss you,
But we'll be okay.
You're going to see your Mamma again,

And your Daddy,
And my brother Seth too.
They're all waiting for you."

I felt him squeeze my hand,
I felt him relax a little.

Then I said,
"Your best friend Dave
is coming from California on Wednesday.
He'll be here Thursday.
He's coming to see you."

And I felt him relax a little more.

The wild waving he had been doing
Since he got so sick
Had stopped.

He seemed more at peace now.
My Daddy,
My Daddy who fought so many demons
 his whole life,
The death of his mother when he was only five,
The death of his only son when his son was just
twenty-three.

But my Daddy, though silent much of the time,
Because of his grief,
Was never cruel,
Was rarely cross.

He was sweet
And loving
And special.

He loved to read his dental journals
He loved to play tennis
And bike ride
And jog.

And when he was too sick to jog
He loved to walk.

And when he was too sick to walk
He loved to talk about physical fitness.

I remember the time he drove out to
a parking lot on Long Island
because the radio show I hosted
could not be heard in Queens.

And he sat in that parking lot
And listened to my show.

I remember how he flew to London
to see where his darling daughter Eileen was living.
But he only stayed a day
Because his wife and lifetime companion
Could not come.
So he did not care about London,
He just wanted to come home to his beloved Glady.

I remember my Daddy
And I know how much he loved his family
His wife
His children
His grandchildren
His brother, his in-laws, and his cousins.

And I know, as does anyone who knew my Daddy,
that there were two Bill Barkas's—
the one before my brother's death,
and the one after.

Before, he smiled and laughed
and had some fun,
and filled his letters with words like

"bubbly, buoyant, brimming with enthusiasm,
energy, and effervescent…"
Afterwards, he was a sad man.
Nothing could take away that sadness.
He tried to be there for all of us.
He lasted more than 80 years.
But a part of him died back then in 1969,
A big part of him.
We could not make it up to him,
No matter how hard we tried.

And I don't blame my Daddy for that
for he loved his son
and he lost his son
and he punished himself for that loss
even though it had to do with bad luck
and not bad parenting.

Good-bye, Daddy.
I'll miss you.
I'll never forget you.
I have the letters you penned,
I have the phrases you said or wrote to me.

The last words you said to me,
before you could not speak,

when I asked you your
favorite color,
You said, "Red."
That day you told Mommy,
"You are pretty."

I'm going to think of you in heaven,
healthy again,
playing tennis on the
Angel Doubles Team,
as your Mommy and Daddy
cheer you on,
As Seth writes it up for the
Angel News.

Daddy, you will always be my hero.
I have been blessed by your love.
Those who were fortunate to know you
Were blessed by your love,
Your friendship,
Your example.

You spent 54 years with your loving bride,
Your love so strong,
such a model for your
children and all who knew you.

You were best friends with Dave for 75 years,
Since kindergarten.
A friendship so solid,
an ideal for us all.

You were a dentist and fought in World War II.
You got malaria, but you survived.
But this illness was a battle
You could not win.
Your spirit was willing
But your body was failing.

Rest in peace, my caring, sincere,
and one-of-a-kind Daddy,
Rest in peace.

Getting Used to Life without Dad

It's been just three weeks
Since Dad went away
to a better place,
Some will say.
I don't say better,
I just say away,
It has been three weeks
Since that fateful day.

It seems much longer,
Much longer still,
Since I danced with my Daddy
Or talked and walked, too
Yet the days at the beach
Those very distant days,
Somehow those days seem much closer
The days when I was two.

But now,
The time seems so strange
As I struggle to readjust my world
Again and again.

I do not have a father anymore.

Never again will I hear his voice
Or see his smile.
Never again will I hear his praise
Or feel like his little child.

But this new life,
I will somehow make it good,
This new life,
I will somehow make it work.

There are so many there for me,
My Husband,
        Children,
                Mother,
Sister,
        Friends,
                Extended family.
Dog,
        Cats,
                Frogs,
Nephews,
        Nieces,
                Cousins,
Aunts,
        Uncles,
                Neighbors.

Computer,
  Paint brush,
    Desk,
House,
  Car,
    Writing,
Consulting,
  Dreams,
    Memories.

But oh how I miss my Dad!
Oh how I long for the days we never had.

No, I cannot be self-indulgent
I cannot look back,
I must look forward.

It seems so weird
So sad and bewildering.
It will take time to adjust
I must give myself some time.

Time to mourn,
Time to let his death sink in.
For I keep expecting him to walk through the
door,

Or walk up the hill from our house,
And wait for my children
As they get off the school bus,
As he did so many times.

I still expect my Dad to call me
Or to answer the phone when I call him
And to ask if I really called to speak to my
mother.

Now I cannot speak to Dad
And I wish I had called more often.
But I know he was proud
And I know he was fulfilled
In his soft-spoken, humble way.

Are you at peace, Bill Barkas?
We miss you down here,
But we know you will always
Be in our thoughts, in our hopes,
In our dreams.

Take care, Dad.
I'll write again, soon.
Got to help you to keep your
Angel Scrapbook filled up

With the thoughts and wishes
Of your loved ones down here.

Bye, for now, sweet father.

I Saved a Moth Today

I saved a moth today,
Instead of killing it,
I let it fly away.

First I chased the moth around
both high and low and up and down.
All through the house it flew
Where it went, I never knew.

It wasn't even hurting me
Although my closet it did see.
But I got there just before
And very gently closed the door.

It felt so good to save that moth.
Even though it tried to eat my cloth.
Having the power over death and life.
Me with my swatter ready to strike.

But I chose not to use this power of mine.
Even though I knew that all would be fine.
Instead I guided the moth to where it could fly.
Out the back door to its freedom in the sky.

It was a day for joy, not a day to cry.
It certainly was no time for a moth to die.

Missing You

Last night Mom babysat
Even though the boys are not
Babies anymore.

She looked so beautiful
Your wife
Your love
Your best friend.

You would have been
Proud of her Dad.

She's trying so hard
To be there for me
For us
Now that you're gone
And She is the only one
Who can be there.

But Mom's not you
And I still miss you
That special Father-daughter
Bond we had

The bond that made Mom so jealous
So afraid
So resentful.

Wasn't it silly
Now that you're gone
And that's all behind us?

Wasn't it a waste of time,
Love,
Energy,
Effort,
Memories,
Dreams,
Comfort
To have two of the three
Women in your life
In competition over you?

And why was my sister never
A competitor?

I wish we could
Have worked all that out
Before you died, Dad,
But alas it's been worked out

Since you're gone.

He was there last night.
Mom's new boyfriend.
You'd like him, Dad.
He's a nice guy.
Served in World War II,
Just like you,
Loves and worships Mom,
Just like you did.

She needs that love
She needs that worship
She needs that attention.

But I miss Her.
I miss the Mom I had during the two years
Between your death and her new boyfriend.

I miss the feeling that
I was number one in Mom's life.
I know it's selfish
I know it's immature
But I got loving and warmth
And the relationship with Mom

I had never really had before.

And I want it again
But I know He's the new
Object of her affection.

And I know one side of me
Is so happy for Mom
That she doesn't have to be all alone
Even though she said it didn't bother her
I know it did
Because she used to tell me
It *didn't* bother her
even without being asked.

So I'm reaching out to you
My Daddy, my sweet Daddy,
I'm reaching out to you in my dreams
In my memories
In my thoughts.

Because I don't want to turn to food
Instead of people
Because I don't want to tune out
Emotionally
Because loving and losing

Is so painful.

So I ask you to stay with me,
Dad, in a stronger way.
Stay with me Dad in
My thoughts

As a source of strength
As a source of joy
Not as a source of sadness
Or regrets.

I know you're at peace
And I want you to know
We're doing okay down here
In this temporary place below.

I found a tape of you and I talking
Just the other day
Your voice was clear and strong
It was as if you were right here
Talking with me.

But it made me miss you even more
Because it is just a tape
Not a person

I could hug
I could look at
I could call up on the phone
Just to say hello.

It was that way you had
Whenever I called
To make me feel that
You *truly* cared that I had called.

It was the way you had
Of making me feel
Whenever we spoke or
Saw eachother
That I was
the most wonderful person
in the world
And you were so glad I was your daughter.

That is what I miss most of all.

And so
I write this poem to you
The first one since you died
Three long years ago.

A poem inspired by seeing Him
Last night
Because He is not you.

But I'll be okay, Dad,
Because you were you
And I will always have you
Within my heart.

Bye for now.

Holidays Are Hard

Each time we celebrate
And you're not there
Each time we commemorate
And you're not there
It's not the same
As when you were part of it.

But it's not the first Father's Day without you
Or the first Thanksgiving or
The first Passover.

No, it's been three years so
We're over all those firsts.

Which makes it all the harder
Since I can't even say
"The first Passover without Dad."

It was a nice evening
But it could not be perfect
With you gone.

If you could join us

For even one more holiday
I would memorize every single
Moment about you and
About that day.

What you said
And what you wore.
What you talked about
And what you thought.

I would create more memories
For me and Fred and the kids.
More memories to cherish
About the Grandpa, the Father who's gone.

But we didn't have enough warning
And I feel now we squandered
Too many times
Too many years
Too many holidays.

The food was fine tonight
And no one got angry
And there were no fights.

But I just couldn't seem to connect to Mom or

to her new boyfriend
As I could connect with you.

And I could see her boyfriend
Was not all that interested
When I bragged, yes bragged, about
What I was doing.

When I told You about
What I was doing
It never seemed like bragging.

But it did with him.

I miss being able to
connect in just a glance
The way you and I did, Dad.

And I try to talk with her boyfriend
But I'm still too needy
To get to know him
I'm still trying to get the
Same reaction from him that
You always gave me.

The love in your eyes.

The adoring look of a father
Amazed that you and your wife
Created this wonderful child.

That's how you always made me feel, Dad,
Just with a glance
Just with your voice.

There was none of that from Mom
or Him tonight
At least I felt connected to my husband
And my kids
And my cats.

And at least the food was okay
And I didn't have to order in this year
Because I was too stressed out
To cook.

So it was a good holiday
A festive holiday
But I needed to let you know
That you're not forgotten.
Even though we all go on our
Merry ways
Trying to act like "life goes on."

Even though one life did end when
You died.

Yes, life has gone on.
Life goes on,
But it's not the same life.

If I wear down a pair of shoes,
I can give away the pair
And get new ones.

If I get into an argument
With a close friend
It's very sad and traumatic
But I manage to get over it.

If I outgrow an outfit,
Whether it's too big or too small.
I reluctantly get a new one.

But you, Dear Father,
You cannot be replaced.
Not in a billion, trillion years.

That gave you your power

In my life.
That gave you the place you had
And will always have
As I try to fill the void

As I try to live each moment more completely
And somehow try to get to know Mom more
While I still have the chance.

Trying to Get Along With Mom

Why is it every time
I try to share my feelings
We end up shouting at each other?

Why is it every time
I want you to understand me
We end up with you announcing
That you don't want to "burden me"
 with your problems?

I spent so many years
As a child
Afraid of you.

I spent so many years
Keeping my feelings to myself
Sad, lonely, putting
You before me.

That silence had consequences

To me and
To others that I loved.

I will be silent no more.

But must we fight when I speak?
Is there no middle ground
Between phony pleasantries
And shouting or screaming?

I will not overeat when I want to speak.
I will not be silent when I need to share.

"I'm not giving up trying to
communicate with you,"
I said to you, shaking,
"You're all I have now that
Daddy's gone
So I'm going to try to
Find a way to communicate with you."

There is adrenaline rushing
Through my arms
My veins
My heart.

"Stop living in your childhood,"
you say back to me.
I try to explain
I'm not reliving my childhood
I'm just trying to understand it
And get past it.

But I wish I *did* want to relive it
I wish it had been pleasant enough to relive.

I know I relive the three weeks from
When I met Fred till our wedding.

I get great pleasure reliving every moment
From the letter he sent to me
When he answered my personal ad
To the first time I called him
And heard his voice.

I relive the first date
And the second date
And the first present he gave me,
A book by Elmore Leonard,
A hardcover book he tracked down
In an out-of-print shop.

It was such a special gift
Because Fred loves Elmore Leonard novels
And he wanted me to share what he loved.

And that was the first sign that he wanted
Me to share his life.

And we did
Just two weeks later
Begin sharing our life
And we've kept sharing it

And it's caring
And loving
And we've also shared the losses:
Of Fred's father
Of my Father
Of my aunt
Of Fred's cousin
Of Fred's uncle.

And the births
Of our two sons,
Of my brother's grandson
Of Fred's sibling's children.

So, dear Mother,
I *wish* I wanted to relive my childhood.

Memories, good memories,
Are okay to relive.

I'll admit that emotionally I am stuck
 in my childhood
Because it's hard to relive the joy
Through the pain.

I won't stop trying to get close to you Mom.
Trying in person
Trying over the phone.
Trying in writing
Trying in poetry.

You're my one and only Mother
And I want..I need…you to
Understand me
Not just love me because
I'm your daughter.

I need you to love *me*
The way my Daddy always did.

My Late Brother's Son Turns 30 Today

My brother's son turns thirty today
The son he never knew.
My brother was just twenty-three
When he was killed
By those sociopath enraged teens
Who singled him out
On that dark cold February night
For no other reason
Than that he was "white."

Ironic it would always be
That they singled him out for their rage
A boy who championed the poor
A man who raised money for causes
A young filmmaker and writer with
Friends of every color and religion.

They singled out the wrong one to hate
They took away the life of a promising talent
They took away the father of his adopted son
They denied his wife a husband

They denied his son a father
They took away my brother
They took away my parents' son.

Once there were three in my family,
Two sisters and a brother,
Then, one sad day in February, there
Were only two.

I have spent the second half of my life
Without a brother.
I have tried these thirty years to
Love my sister
To always remember my nephew
The son my brother never saw
The son who looks so much like my brother
But who has no memory of him.

There's a song that Cher sings that goes
"If I could turn back time"
And if I could, I would
To that day
So many years ago
When Seth went out to review a play
And he ended up in Bellevue's emergency room,
Knife wounds in his back and side.

It would have a different outcome.
Instead of my mother telling my sister and me
that it was time to say good-by
 to my comatose brother
I would be sitting on a chair
 next to his hospital bed
Surrounded by dozens of flower bouquets and
balloons saying "get well soon."

And we would joke about his close call.
We could joke about having one to tell his kids
about the night that gang approached him and
asked him for a dime
And pulled out a knife instead.

But instead of what happened
Seth would be victorious.
He would be the one to walk away.
They would get arrested.
The gang might even get beaten up
But Seth would not be harmed,
Seth would not be dead.

There are some losses that are so sad
So painful and so cruel.

Death of course happens to us all,
Sooner or later,
But when it's sooner,
And when it's cruel,
It's hard to be an upbeat happy-go-lucky type.
When you see what's going on in Kosovo
And you personally experienced the same kind
of viciousness against your brother
So many years ago
When you personally saw the results of
The kind of cruelty few will ever know.

My brother's son grew up without him
And now he has a girlfriend
And his girlfriend has a 5-year-old child
Just like when my brother met
his future wife and she had
A son, Ariel, who was then called Kenny,
And my brother adopted him,
And thought of him as his own.

And Kenny lost a father
And his biological son was in
His wife's womb when
The fatal blows were struck
And two months later

His son was born.

My brother told me how excited he
Was about becoming a father
And how scared he was about
Being about to support another child.
He was considering getting a teaching job
Giving up the freelance life
But it all ended
In just a few moments
On a cold East Village street
At 11 o'clock at night
One freezing February night
Thirty years ago.

And they say that there's fewer
Crimes when it's very cold
Because the criminals don't like
To be on the streets when it's that cold.

They were wrong.
Dead wrong.

Goodbye, Dr. Leeds, My Psychological Guru

I can't believe I'm writing this poem
Instead of calling you on the phone.
I can't believe that you're gone
And that
never again
will you ask
me,
"How're you doing?"
So I could say, "Fine."

For the last fourteen years
You have been my
Good mother
     Good father
          Good brother
               Good sister
                    Good friend
Good therapist
     Good teacher
          Good mentor
You have been my psychological guru.

When someone asked if I was seeing a

therapist,
I would reply,
"Yes, but I really think of him as my
psychological guru."

Dr. Leeds, I have learned so much from
you
So much that I never before knew.

I learned how to love *unconditionally*
I learned how to feel bona fide joy and
how to truly cry.
I learned how to grieve
And I learned how to let myself feel
pain and sadness
when someone I love dies.

I finally learned to feel the feelings
So I could lose the weight.

I learned to forgive myself
And to mourn the childhood I never
had.

I learned how to never give up on
anyone I love

No matter how wrong
No matter how sad
No matter how much they make me angry or
mad.

I learned the strength of good feelings
And the fear those good feelings could bring,
And the power of honesty and truth
And the glory of being me,
Lose, draw, or win.

I learned about commitment and caring
And feeling someone truly knows and
appreciates me
The way I had always hoped someone would.

You were so sensitive, so insightful, so real
You were not afraid of words or feelings
or even the oddest dreams that I could share
for it was in your amazing interpretation of
dreams
that your true genius revealed itself, ever so rare.

Dr. Leeds, you are irreplaceable,
You who helped so many,
You who cared so much.

You were the best your profession could offer
And I will carry within me and through those I
love and know
All the values that you taught me.

My children benefit from what you tutored me
My marriage is richer because of the insights I
gained.

Because of you, and the work we did together,
the cycle of frustration will not be repeated
The emotional depravation I felt growing up
Stops with my generation.

I am able to give to my family the love,
Understanding, caring, and sacrifice,
All the qualities you gave to me.

There are so many lessons you shared:
"If you have a choice between the hard way
and the easy way, choose the hard way,"
you would say.
"You pay now or later."
 "Even prizefighters get two minutes off between
rounds."

You taught me that you don't directly change
others. You change yourself and others may then
change as well.

But even more than the phrases that summed up
Your philosophies and miraculous insight into
human nature
What I think of most of all
When I think back on the myriad of lessons
You helped me to learn
Was the uncanny way you were able to make me
feel
that *I* was your only patient,
That for the length of our session,
that *I* was the only one that counted.

Yet I knew you cared about so many others--
patients as well as your family
 outside of your practice.
But it was your gift to stay focused on just *me*
When it was my time.
Even if you shared an example,
An anecdote, or a story,
It was always in your role as
My psychological guru
As you gave me that total focus,

that healthy egocentricity
That helps someone take on the world
And become all she or he could be.

Dr. Leeds, my psychological guru,
my role model,
I will think of you up above,
Meeting my brother Seth for the first time,
The brother I told you so much about
As you also greet my father
who died three long years ago.

It gives me comfort to think of you writing and
editing the Psychology column
 in the *Angel News,*
The newspaper I like to think that my brother
Started when he got to heaven 30 years ago.

Dr. Leeds, you'll help all those angels
To realize their goals.
You'll help them to see
if they're getting too ethereal.

You were an anchor that grounded me
And so many others for so very long
But now we must all fly on our own.

Now we must soar from the inner strength
that you helped us to find
because you cared
because you dared
To be one in a trillion.

Dr. David Leeds,
My therapist,
My mentor,
My friend.

I can hear you saying to me,
After I share this poem,
"You're terrific."

It is that self-love
and an enhanced ability to connect with others
That you inspired in me
That I will now continue to carry on
Throughout my life.
Giving it to myself
And to others
As well as through my work,
As a testimony to you and to your career.

There are so many of us

Who are more fulfilled and self-aware
Because we were blessed to have you
As our psychological guru.

I am so sorry I did not say goodbye to you
 so I will say it now, "Goodbye, Dr. Leeds."

Rest in peace
Knowing that those you helped
Are forever more peaceful
Because of you.

A Post-Grief (and Angry) Second Goodbye

When I first learned mypsychological guru
 had died I felt deep grief
So deep I wailed when his associate called me
with the news.

Wailed from the deepest part of me
From my inner core

From a place of love and caring that I have
opened up these years
Largely because of Him.

But then, without even thinking about it,
Anger took over.

Anger
      Rage
            Regrets
                  Despair.

All the unanswered questions
As I realize my therapist was
First and foremost a man.

A man with failings
A man who was frail
A man who gave us the best of him.

But he didn't share about his cancer
He didn't share about his pain.

He didn't tell us he was dying
When confronted he said it was laryngitis.

But I knew it was cancer.
I knew, deep down, he was dying.

But I didn't go to see him
I spoke on the phone.

It was easier
It was kinder
It was more convenient.

But I had to drive to the funeral
I had to finally make the drive that I thought was
too far all those years.

And it wasn't all that far.

It was an hour away
And I could have gone there before.

But I was afraid.
Afraid to be alone in the house with him
Even though it had seemed so safe
All those years I saw him in Manhattan
When he had his Park Avenue office for
Some thirty years.

I only saw him in Manhattan for about five years
But it felt safe.

It didn't feel safe in his home
On Long Island.

So we did phone therapy
And I got a lot out of it
But we weren't face to face.

And I have always been afraid of face to face
So I hid behind my fear
Using the excuse that Long Island was too far.

Now I wonder who those phone calls were more

convenient for,
Him or me?

Who was hiding?
Who kept more secrets?

In the end, I think I gave him
More than he gave me.

In the end, I embodied his values
And lived his ideals
More than he did.

In the end,
His patients represented the best of him,
An enigma till the end.

But it didn't have to be that way.

Or did it?

I am without a therapist now.

I am doing self-therapy.

But I still have my husband

My children
My mother
My sister
My friends
My cats
My work
My home
My hobbies
My books
My computer
My "cyberfriends"
My speaking friends
My memories
My talents.

But most of all I have my calm.

To him, I owe that calm.

He helped me find an inner calm
Even if he could not find it for himself.

But I will always wonder why he denied his
death.
Why he had to lie and tell us he had laryngitis
When he was really dying of cancer.

Why?
Why?
Why?

Perhaps that is the lesson he has taught me,
even in his death,
That if I can accept his imperfection
Maybe I can finally forgive my mother
 for being less than perfect

For he did try his best, I know he did,
So didn't she always try her best as well?

To forgive him, and to forgive her,
Is to forgive myself.

Farewell, John, John
Brave Little Boy, Man-Hero to Millions

We'll always remember your brave salute
So mature
So powerful
So telling
When your father,
 the beloved late President Kennedy,
Was felled by an assassin's bullet
That dark day in November 1963.

It is etched in our minds
It is engraved in our memories
A brave little boy
Forced to deal with loss and fame
So young
So soon.

But outside the eyes of the public
You grew up
And suddenly you were a heartthrob to so many
So handsome
So successful
So witty
So self-deprecating

The hope of so many generations.

A son of the City
Tribeca and New York claimed you
Massachusetts was a part of you too.

But suddenly a cruel twist of fate
A doomed flight
A downed plane
And three lives are lost.

Three lives of promise
Three lives of hope.

The young man whom so many had hoped
would someday follow
In your father's footsteps
To provide us with a President to emulate
To admire
To worship.

The beautiful wife you loved
With whom we all hoped you would someday
have children
To pass on your legacy.

Your sister-in-law
A bright light in investment banking
With a romantic future
Still in the making.

In an instant
All gone.

The hopes
The dreams
The jokes
The humor
The history
The present
The future.

I mourn your death, John F. Kennedy Jr.,
and the loss of your wife and sister-in-law.
Although I did not know you personally
You were and always will be part of my world.

A world diminished because you three
Are no longer part of it.

I will miss hearing about you
I will miss seeing what you are up to

The fashion that your wife was wearing
The causes you were championing.

Just as we miss Princess Diana
And all she meant to the world
we will miss you three,
Struck down so young, still in your prime.

There is no lesson we can learn from this
Except to cherish each moment
To always let those we love know of our love.
To follow our dreams
And feel the feelings,
Make the connections--
With our family
Our friends
Our work
Our dreams.

You touched our lives with your life.
You have jolted and shocked us in your death.

For you seemed larger than life
You seemed able to overcome anything and
everything
You were so poised when your beloved mother

Jacqueline succumbed to cancer

We will never know how you would have aged
How you would have changed
What you might have done
What you might have been
For a page in history has ended.

John, John,
I salute you
As you find the eternal peace
 with your loved ones
That you deserve.

Ode to my Unborn Child

I try not to think of you
The baby I never knew
I try to put it out of my mind
What you would have been—
Boy, girl, intelligent, kind?

But then someone gracious,
My friend Nona,
Reminds me that I am not the only one who
Mourns your loss.

My friend Nona reminds me that others
Feel my pain   .
The pain of loss
The pain of regret
About the unborn child
The fetus lost at 9 weeks
Lost and I may never know why.

I remember how hard it was when I knew you were gone
How I wailed in the doctor's office
Moaned from my deepest being
When the doctor said there was no longer a heart beat.

I was numb
I was sad
I was so devastated.

And then,
When I told others of my pain,
Of my loss,
All they could say was,

"But you already have two healthy children
Be grateful for that"
As if any one life could cancel out another
As of any one life could substitute for another.

But you would have been unique
And we already picked out a name for you—
Michelle, if a girl
Brian, if a boy

And I remember those names
And I remember you
So many years later
For I was the third child
And I know how different
My family and the world would have been
If I had never been born.

But I was born,
I was the third,
So in just a few months, we began to try again,
For we shared the view of those who thought
They had comforted me
When they said, "Try again.
You can have another."

We tried,
We tried so very hard
With charts, with pills,
With injections,
With wishes and hopes.

But fate had another role for me
And so, at the young age of forty-four,

I found I could no longer have children,
Early menopause,
The body stopped producing eggs
Long before the heart,
A heart big enough to love many children
And I know I would have had another child, or two, or more,
And loved each and every one.

But that was not what fate had in store for me.

So I started throwing myself into my work
I started a publishing company
and created books instead of children
And focused on loving the two children we have even more.

And so when someone wonders at the frenzy with which
I create new books
The passion with which I grow my company
I smile and try to remind myself of the source of that drive
Of the need to create new life that was stifled too soon.

Of Michelle or Brian who could not make the journey
But who will never be forgotten
As long as there is a loving friend like Nona
To remind me that she remembers my pain
And empathizes with my loss.

The technical word for it is *miscarriage*
And in so many ways it is a miscarriage—
A miscarriage of justice—
A mistake but one that I did not let defeat me.

But it is important to mourn that loss

Even all these years later
For it was and is a loss
Even if there was no burial
Even if there was no funeral
Even if there were no condolence cards.

I wanted that baby
We all wanted that baby
But he/she was not able to join our family
Yet his/her spirit does live on
In my thoughts, in my dreams,
In my memories, in my drive to create,
In my need to connect intimately
With others, to love and be loved.

Part II

Coping With War

Poems by Fred Yager

Silenced by a Bomb

when one man misuses the power
to take life at a whim
he should either be stripped
of that power
or have life taken from him.

you can't throw a ball that's already tossed
you can't win a war that's already lost.

there's a still wind blowing
through the trees in Vietnam.
it passes leaves unturning
it comes from houses burning
it carries scents of dying
there's no more people crying
they were silenced by a bomb.

Cold Day in Summer

From a hut in Vietnam,
To a shanty in Selma, Alabama.
The cries are all alike,
From the children of dead fathers.
And it just looks like,
 It's gonna be another
 Cold day in summer.

From the campus of Kent State
To the killing fields of hate.
The skies rained black death
While our streets filled with blood.
And it just looks like
 It's gonna be another
 Cold day in Summer.

We tried to love,
But it turned to rage,
Some people died,
Or were put in a cage.

Then we placed the blame
On chosen fate.
Well the war's come home

And it's too late.
And it just looks like,
It's gonna be another,
Cold day in summer.

Like riders in the night,
Armed and ready to fight.
They come to me in dreams,
 Reaching out to spear my soul.
And it just feels like
 it's gonna be another
 Cold day in summer.

 They made us their soldiers,
 To fight to the death.
 But nobody told us,
 About what to do next.

Where are we supposed to go,
When the killing's done?
Go home to face the heartache,
Have a good time, and some fun?

They never told us how to live.
We were just prepared to die

They never taught us how to give.
Just to kill, or be killed with honor.

And it just looks like it's
just gonna be another,
Cold day in summer.

We Won't Go

far from the dead and dying,
away from the orphans crying,
where dead mothers and fathers are lying,
we sit in our tight white homes.

and that's where we're gonna stay
cause we can fight tomorrow
we're gonna love today.
it's the right thing to do.
it's the American way.
don't do what we do,
do what we say.
our leaders will set us straight,
you know they will.
our doctors will make death late,
and lower their bill.
but now, yeah now,
right now is the time
for all to know
that war is a crime
and we won't go.

hell no, we won't go

pulling life down low
to make widows and orphans
and help poverty grow.

Part III
Mourning
Poems By Priscilla Orr

An Odd Elegy for my Mom*

After an all night rain the sand clings to everything.
Shrimp boats are anchored for winter, their paint
   peeling.
Even my coffee's bitter. Why come back
to this ratty brown shore you loved. Why talk to you
as if you weren't dead. Last night, I hunted down
my old academy. No white stone building
--just a lot full of old oak and pecan trees.
No ghost of Sister Leonard, whistle click against her
      beads.
No ghost of a girl in a blue pleated skirt, scuffed
      oxfords.

My ex-husband has MS, a virus that gnaws away
 the myelin coating of the nerve. Scar tissue hardens
over raw wound, all damage hidden until the ravage
      ends.
He can never know if he'll see again, or know
where the virus might erupt next,
his own immune system poised to destroy him.

If I throw this cup away, it will decompose
only into tiny beads of Styrofoam

that slip into the gullet of a catfish or crab.
My friend drinks two gallons of wine without
    stopping,
and I succumb in my own way, drink a toast to you.

Here's to you, my mom, if you can hear me.
Here's to this salt water Gulf that gets us all.

*Reprinted, with permission, from *Jugglers and Tides: Poems* by Priscilla Orr (Stamford, CT: Hannacroix Creek Books, 1997), p. 64.

Grief*

In winter, the Chinook winds lifted snow
from the bushes and deposited it
outside our basement apartment window.

These drifts blocked the evening sun
 but for one fragment of light spilled
 into the living room. I could hear

the cab door slam, your boots crunch
up the walk. After the snowfall --
ruts, dog urine, boot prints all froze.

Before attempting suicide, my friend
told me a memory: she is a child folded
into a living room curtain. She peers

through the venetian blind into the dark
waiting for the orphan wagon -- the man
in crepe soled shoes who steps towards her.

They have shut your eyes, wiped the vomit
from your lips. While I sit next to your bed

a few drops of blood on the sheet turn brown

as they dry. You have quieted yourself,
my slack-faced angel; the mild night wind
fills the room as your cheek begins to cool.

*Reprinted, with permission, from Orr's *Jugglers and Tides* , p. 65.

Part IV

Untitled

A Poem by Seth Alan Barkas

Untitled *

Some day or other I expect to
wake up, down my breakfast
O.J., shift through the apartment
hallway, fumble through the
Amusements and Arts section,
finally glancing at the editorials
which I never read and the
obituaries to see which prominent
people have died . . . and find
my name in bold face type
somewhere on the page, calmly
informing my classmates from
wherever that my time has come
and gone.

I didn't think about this
too much until Don McNeil
died. I didn't know Don but
then friends of mine who write
for the *Voice* were always mentioning

*Seth Alan Barkas was a 23-year-old freelance writer at the time of his death, working as the film critic for *Baltimore Magazine* and reviewing plays for *Show Business* newspaper.

how good a writer he was.
About my age, 23, a revolutionary
journalist. The kind of person
people called sensitive. So
he's swimming up in Monroe,
New York and he's wiped out.
And I think, I used to live
during the summers in Greenwood Lake,
 about 12 miles from
Monroe, and I'm a journalist but
more revolutionary in thought
than action but I haven't been
wiped out.

For about one week, I thought
about Don McNeil. Casually
reminded of his fate by poems
and prose in the *Voice*, but
nothing more shocking than
his *Times* obit. So I
promised myself and those
around me that things
WILL BE DIFFERENT. I'm
going to start living for

the day, the moment, the instant.
Everything for love and
happiness. No more suffering,
no more work, tomorrow, tomorrow,
no more tomorrows — my edition
might be late. But I don't
change, I just worry more.

Then I get word that it
has stricken again. Ignominiously,
without even an obit in the
Times. No one
will write of him.

He was one of my best friends
when I was about 12 years
old. He liked to steal and he taught
me to steal, even though we were
almost affluent kids in Queens.
I was the lookout for a three
pen heist of a Queens
Department store (and almost
wet my pants) and once
payed for a two-bit
wallet clipped from a department store
in Jamaica . . .

He taught me the little
bit I know about race hatred,
not that he was a bigot, he
was just an elementary school
troublemaker and he called
the only slib teacher in
the whole damn school
"chocolate baby." It
made everyone laugh. But
otherwise—her name was
of all things Mrs. Robinson —
she liked him. Because despite
his dislike for almost everything
from teachers to people,
there was something genuinely
nice about him.

He used to steal me bike
parts and I'd pay him with
the trains my parents bought
me but in which I was no longer
interested. He was the first
kid I knew to buy an air gun,
and he promptly plugged a number
of holes in our junior high

school with it, and shot a
bird in my backyard, which
I didn't approve of.

He was a mechanical genius.
He'd steal a hundred dollar
watch just to take it apart,
often failing to put it back
together again. He'd fix
anything broken you could give
him, from a burned out radio
to a bike siren that wouldn't
screech.

He was a damn good fighter,
but while he was one of the
toughest kids about our
neighborhood he took pity on
my ego complex — not that he
ever let me beat him, he just
gently made me give. He made
me give ten times in a row.
He made me give even after
I put on some Paratrooper
boots that made my feet hurt
and went out to kick the shit

out of him. He made me give,
and he made me cry.

He took me out into the
woods and showed me dirty
books ≡ a girlie magazine,
before it printed words. He
took me down the cellar
of the basement of some stores
and with two other girls,
in the dark, amidst the rats,
he made strange sounds as
did his girl. Mine quietly
trembled along side me until
everything was over.

He taught me, with some other
guys, how to gamble on the corner
without my father finding out;
how to start smoking at eight
years old and call the smoke,
which we stole from parents,
wood for an unknown reason.

And he liked to build

in that fantastic
wood that is so much a brocade
of our lives — the park next
to the junior high
school in Queens where we built everything
from tree houses to caves —

But growing up separated
us. I went to high school.
He went to trade school —
always in and out of trouble,
his mischief getting progressively
worse until the only messages
about him I would hear would
mention that he had been sent
up.
Until the most recent one.
In the woods of our youth,
He was discovered,
dead at 24 years, with an
overdose of heroin. It happened;
jumbling my memories. I'm
not sure he was a "good"
person, but I liked him. He

was good to me. And whether I
liked him or not, it's unimportant
Sooner or later I'm going to join
him in the great together.
It scares me.

Part V

Coping With the Loss of a Grandparent

A Poem by Scott Yager

95

When Grandpa Came Over

When Grandpa came over he'd mostly sleep
When they would arrive we'd hear a beep.
We all knew his favorite dish was soup
He'd like to watch me shoot a hoop.

I remember when we used to take a walk
It would give us a chance to really talk
We have a pair of wonderful cats
They'd rush in his bedroom and go to sleep in his hats.

He'd go to the store and bring us back lunch
When he'd come home we'd all munch, munch, munch.
Me and him would go into his room to watch "The Price Is Right,"
And we'd hardly ever get into a fight.

For the past few months I've been filled with bore
Just yesterday I realized—
Grandpa won't be coming over anymore.

In 1996, when he was 11 years old, Scott Yager's maternal 80-year-old grandfather, William Barkas, D.D.S., died. Scott wrote this poem at that time and read it at his grandfather's funeral.

Epilogue
Coping With Grief
by Jan Yager, Ph.D.

"A single person is missing for you, and the whole world is empty. But one no longer has the right to say so aloud…" That is how French scholar Philippe Aries summed up the change in how we deal with death and grief in his fascinating treatise *Western Attitudes Toward Death from the Middle Ages* (Baltimore, Maryland: Johns Hopkins University Press, 1974; page 92). I read that book in the 1970s, when I was researching my masters thesis on crime victims as well as my book *Victims* (Scribner's, 1978). Aries' writings had a tremendous impact on my thinking, then and now. He pointed out the dramatic change in how the dying and death were perceived, with the greatest changes occurring between 1930 and 1950 when death would more likely occur alone, in a hospital, rather than at home in the presence of family.

Three other books that have had a tremendous influence on my appreciation of the impact of illness, death, and grief are Elisabeth Kubler-Ross's groundbreaking book, *On Death and Dying* (NY: Macmillan, 1969). Kubler-Ross pinpointed the five stages those who are dying, as well as those closest to the terminally ill, go through upon learning that death is likely: Stage 1 – denial and isolation; Stage 2 – Anger; Stage 3 – Bargaining; Stage 4 – Depression; and Stage 5 – Acceptance.

The next book that helped me to say goodbye to my father when he was dying in the hospital was an incredible book by two nurses who deal with dying patients: *Final Gifts: Understanding the Special Awareness, Needs, and Communications of the Dying* by

Maggie Callanan and Patricia Kelley (NY: Bantam, 1993). Callanan and Kelley explore the world of the dying in an indepth and detailed way based on their extensive first-hand experiences dealing with scores of dying patients.

The last book is the bestseller *Tuesdays with Morrie*, an eloquent book by Mitch Albom tracing the lessons he learned about life by spending Tuesdays with his former sociology professor, Morrie Schwartz, an insightful elderly man, who was dying.

Made into a TV movie in December 1999, produced by Oprah Winfrey, the book and the TV movie highlight how much the dying can teach us about living if we just allow ourselves to listen. Albom's book is important for another reason: it indicates how we are reclaiming the death ritual of saying goodbye that Aries pointed out became lost to us as dying and death took place behind the closed doors of the hospital.

The collection of poems in *The Healing Power of Creative Mourning* about terminal illness, death, and coping with grief is my way of saying and sharing "aloud" the feelings that are brought up by illness, death, and grief. Sharing those feelings through poetry, on paper, with oneself, or with others, is just one positive way of coping with those feelings.

There are so many productive ways you can cope with grief, like writing poetry, talking about your feelings, reading poetry, painting, drawing, dancing, or prayer. There are also ways to deal with it that tend to be more negative or self-destructive, like overeating, withdrawal, or dwelling on negative thoughts.

The work of Dr. Joshua Smyth with asthma and arthritis patients over a four month period supports the idea that writing about the illness or death of a loved one led to positive health improvements, including a lower heart rate, lower blood pressure, and improved immune function. (*J. of American Medical Association*, April 1999.)

Certainly this important research will lead to additional studies of other kinds of patients confirming scientifically what anyone who has gone through these painful experiences would attest to through experiential or anecdotal evidence: that writing can be beneficial.

I added to the collection of my own poems the works of four others: my husband Fred, who in the 1960s wrote about his experiences in the face of death during his tour of duty during the Vietnam War; poet Priscilla Orr, whose two poems about death, including coping with her mother's death, are reprinted, with permission, from her complete poetry collection, *Jugglers and Tides* (Stamford, CT: Hannacroix Creek Books, 1997), an Untitled poem by my late brother, Seth; and my son Scott's poem about his grandfather that he read at his grandfather's funeral. Seth's poem deals with the difficulty he was having coping with the death of two young men who were about his age, around 23. One was an acquaintance; the other a childhood friend. The poem is eerily prophetic as Seth expressed his fears about death; it is a bitter irony that he too would die so young, at the age of twenty-three, not that long after he completed this poem, the victim of a senseless and random street mugging and stabbing.

We hope that the poems in this collection inspire you to find your own way to express how you deal with the terminal illness or the death of a loved one, and your grief, whether through writing, through art, through setting up a memorial fund, an award, a scholarship, holding an annual contest, planting a tree, or creating an organization in your loved one's memory.

Just one of the amazing ironies about coping with terminal illness as well as the death of a loved one is that these experiences, although intensely personal and individual, are universal as well.

In the Selected Bibliography and Resources sections that follow you will find additional books listed that might help children or adults to better cope with the illness or death of a loved one.

Selected Bibliography

On Dying and Death (for adults)

Albom, Mitch. *Tuesdays With Morrie*. New York: Doubleday, 1997. (TV movie version produced by Oprah Winfrey, broadcast on ABC-TV, Sunday, December 5, 1999.)

Aries, Philippe. *The Hour of Our Death*. Translated from the French by Helen Weaver. New York: Vintage Books, 1982.

Aries, Philippe. *Western Attitudes Toward Death from the Middle Ages to the Present*. Translated by Patricia M. Ranum. Baltimore, MD: Johns Hopkins University Press, 1975.

Babwin, Don, Associated Press. "Stress Writing May Ease Pain." reprinted at www.abcnews.go.com/sections/living/DailyNews/writing_health990413.html 4/16/99)

Brody, Jane E. "When a Loss Remains Unresolved." *New York Times*, March 23, 1999, p. F1, F2.

Callanan, Maggie and Patricia Kelley. *Final Gifts*. New York: Bantam, 1993.

Davies, Phyllis. *Grief: Climb Toward Understanding*. San Luis Obispo, CA: Sunnybank Publishers, 1987, 1998.

Goodman, Lisl M. *Death and the Creative Life*. New York: Springer, 1981.

Hendin, David. *Death as a Fact of Life*. New York: Norton, 1973.

Kubler-Ross, Elisabeth. *On Death and Dying*. New York: Macmillan, 1969.

Kushner, Harold. *When Bad Things Happen to Good People*.

New York: Avon Books, 1983.

Shaw, Eva. *What to Do When a Loved One Dies*. Irvine, CA: Dickens Press, 1994.

Schneidman, Edwin S., editor. *Death: Current Perspectives*. Palo Alto, CA: Mayfield Publishing Company, 1976.

Yager,Jan(a/k/a J.L.Barkas) *Friendshifts®: The Power of Friendship and How It Shapes Our Lives* (Stamford, CT: Hannacroix Creek Books, 1997; 2nd edition, 1999). See pages 152-158, "When Someone Close to You or to Your Friend Dies."

_____. "The ulimate loss no family should have to endure." *Catholic Twin Circle* ,June7, 1981, pages 4, 20.

_____. *Victims*. New York: Scribner's, 1978. (2nd edition, in preparation, Hannacroix Creek Books, 2000).

Widowhood

Caine, Lynn. *Widow*. New York: Bantam Books, 1975.

Loss of a Parent

LeShan, Eda. *Learning to Say Good-by: When a Parent Dies*. New York: Macmillan, 1976.

Pet loss

Davis, Christine. *For Every Dog an Angel.* Portland, OR: Lighthearted Press, 1997.

For children

Brown, Laurie Krasny and Marc Brown. *When Dinosaurs Die: A Guide to Understanding Death.* Boston: Little, Brown and Company, 1996.

Buscaglia, Leon. *The Fall of Freddie the Leaf.* New York: Henry Holt, 1982.

Greenlee, Sharon. *When Someone Dies.* Illustrated by Bill Drath. Atlanta, GA: Peachtree, 1992.

Rofes, Eric E. and the Unit at Fayerweather Street School. *The Kids' Book about Death and Dying By and For Kids.* Boston, MA: Little, Brown and Company, 1985.

Shriver, Maria. *What's Heaven?* Illustrated by Sandra Speidel. Golden Books, 1999.

Spero, Moshe Halevi. *Saying Goodbye to Grandpa.* Illustrated by Marilyn Hirsh. New York: Pitsopany Press Inc., 1997.

Stein, Sara Bonnett. *About Dying.* New York: Walker and Company, 1974.

Resources*

There are numerous resources for information or referrals to direct help for coping with terminal illness, death, or grief. Here are a selection of associations, including their mailing and web site addresses, for further information or referrals.

American Association of Retired Persons (AARP)
601 E Street, NW
Washington, D.C. 20049
http://www.aarp.org

American Cancer Society
1599 Clifton Road, NE
Atlanta, Georgia 30329-4251

Americans for Better Care of the Dying
2175 K Street, NW
Suite 820
Washington, D.C. 20037
http://www.abcd-caring.com

American Hospice Foundation
1130 Connecticut Avenue, NW
Suite 700
Washington, D.C. 20036-4101
http://www.americanhospice.org

*Please note that addresses, web sites, and even names change and therefore the accuracy of these listings cannot be guaranteed.

Association for Death Educational and Counseling
638 Prospect Avenue
Hartford, CT 06105

Candelighters Childhood Cancer Foundation
7910 Woodmont Avenue
Suite 460
Bethesda, MD 20814-3015
http://www.candelighters.org

Center for Hope
1003 Post Road
Darien, CT 06820

Children's Hospice International
2202 Mt. Vernon Avenue
Suite 3C
Alexandria, VA 22301
http://www.chionline.org

Compassionate Friends, Inc.
P.O. Box 3696
Oak Brook, IL 60522-3696
http://www.compassionatefriends.org

The Doug Center
P.O. Box 86582
Portland, OR 97286
http://www.dougy.org

Gilda's Club
195 W. Houston Street
New York, New York 10014
http://www.gildasclub.org

GriefNet
http://griefnet.org

Hospice Foundation of America
2001 S Street, NW
Suite 300
Washington, D.C. 20009
http://www.hospicefoundation.org

National Hospice and Palliative Care Organization
1700 Diagonal Road, Suite 300
Alexandria, VA 22314
http://www.nho.org

National Organization of Parents of Murdered Children, Inc.
100 East Eighth Street, B-41
Cincinnati, OH 45202
http://www.pomc.org

Pen-Parents, Inc.
P.O. Box 8738
Reno, NV 89507-8738
http://www.penparents.org

Tragedy Assistance Program for Survivors, Inc. (TAPS)
2001 S Street, NW
Suite 300
Washington, D.C. 20009
http://www.taps.org

ABOUT THE AUTHORS

Jan Yager is the author of more than a dozen books including nonfiction works (*Victims, Friendshifts®, Business Protocol, The Help Book,* and *Creative Time Management for the New Millennium),* a novel, *Untimely Death,* co-authored with her husband Fred, and a children's book, *The Cantaloupe Cat* (illustrated by Mitzi Lyman). She has a Ph.D. in sociology from the City University of New York, an M.A. in criminal justice, a B.A. in fine arts, and did a year of graduate work in psychiatric art therapy. Her web site address is: www.JanYager.com.

Fred Yager, who majored in psychology at the City University of New York, was a war correspondent for the Department of Defense, in the Navy for 4 years, and in Vietnam in active combat for 18 months. He then worked at the Associated Press as a reporter, editor, film critic, and entertainment writer for the next 13 years. He now runs the global TV operations for a financial services corporation. Co-author, with his wife Jan Yager, of the novel *Untimely Death* (Hannacroix Creek Books, 1998), he has several screenplays and a musical in development.

Priscilla Orr, author of *Jugglers and Tides: Poems* (Hannacroix Creek Books, 1997), graduated from the University of Montana and has an M.A. from Columbia University's Teachers College and an M.F.A. from Warren Wilson College. A New Jersey Council on the Arts fellowship recipient, Orr was raised in Mississippi and Montana. On the faculty of a New Jersey college, her poetry has been published in *Southern Poetry Review, Bitterroot International Poetry,* and *Croton Review.*

Seth Alan Barkas was a freelance theatre reviewer for *Show Business* newspaper and movie critic for *Baltimore* magazine at the time he was mugged and killed, the victim of a random street crime, in 1969 at the age of twenty-three. A graduate of New York University, where he was feature editor of the college newspaper, Seth worked as a TV reporter at WBAL-TV in Baltimore. An aspiring playwright and filmmaker, his collected plays are being published by Hannacroix Creek Books, Inc. under the title *In the Great Together*; the cover art for that collection is from a painting by his widow Karen.

Scott Yager is a high school student who enjoys acting, writing, reading, wrestling, and spending time with his friends. He also uses his video camera to make short films. He wrote the poem in this collection, "When Grandpa Came Over," when he was 11 years old, upon learning that his beloved 80-year-old grandfather, who had been terminally ill with a brain tumor for several months before, had died. He read the poem at his grandfather's funeral.